#SUCCESSFUL CORPORATE LEARNING **tweet**
Book04
Career Transition Training and Services That Work in Today's Environment

By Barbara Safani and Mitchell Levy

THiNKaha®

E-mail: info@thinkaha.com
20660 Stevens Creek Blvd., Suite 210
Cupertino, CA 95014

Published by *THiNKaha*®, a Happy About® imprint
20660 Stevens Creek Blvd., Suite 210, Cupertino, CA 95014
http://thinkaha.com

First Printing: April 2012
Paperback ISBN: 978-1-61699-086-2 (1-61699-086-4)
eBook ISBN: 978-1-61699-087-9 (1-61699-087-2)
Place of Publication: Silicon Valley, California, USA
Paperback Library of Congress Number: 2012932531

Trademarks

All terms mentioned in this book that are known to be trademarks or service marks have been appropriately capitalized. Neither Happy About®, nor any of its imprints, can attest to the accuracy of this information. Use of a term in this book should not be regarded as affecting the validity of any trademark or service mark.

Warning and Disclaimer

Every effort has been made to make this book as complete and as accurate as possible. The information provided is on an "as is" basis. The author(s), publisher, and their agents assume no responsibility for errors or omissions. Nor do they assume liability or responsibility to any person or entity with respect to any loss or damages arising from the use of information contained herein.

Advance Praise

"This book is a must read for anyone in Human Resources as well as Management in understanding the importance of providing career transition and support to employees who will be downsized. These are important concepts—not only in order to support the departing employees but to ensure that the remaining employees know how much your company is doing to support their colleagues in these difficult situations. Additionally, as the economy and job markets continue to rapidly change, providing this support to ensure that departing employees are equipped with the skills required to navigate the job search process is crucial. This is an excellent source!"
Ariel Boverman, Board Member, Human Resources Association of New York

"I know Barbara Safani's expertise and solutions work because I have been successfully referring her to my Fortune 100 executive coaching clients for years. The results are always stellar. This new book is another example of her laser-like, practical, and easily implemented advice. I plan to use it and recommend it often. It is written for the way we work and read now, especially in the face of transition."
Angela Love, President, Daymark Group

"Barbara has captured the key aspects of managing a reduction in force in a user-friendly format that can be easily understood and quickly absorbed by both HR professionals and line managers. If you have the unfortunate need to manage a RIF, pick up this book."
Brian McComak, Vice President, Human Resources, Christie's

"Chockfull of clear, concise, and powerful information about the value and importance of career transition services, this 15-minute read transcends HR-speak, giving HR professionals the information they need to gain buy-in for this important benefit. Easily digestible and compelling, this book will make you better able to articulate the benefits of career transition services. In today's short-attention-span learning and working environment, *#SUCCESSFUL CORPORATE LEARNING tweet Book04: Career Transition Training and Services That Work in Today's Environment* is a unique and effective tool."
Jennifer Patterson, SPHR, Director, Human Resources, FOJP Service Corporation

"Barbara continues to impress me with her ability to demonstrate that she is a master of how to manage a downsizing. She provides employers with practical tools to make the process manageable and compassionately provides tips for employees in transition to new careers in a clear and concise manner.

"This book is great and absolutely worth the read for Human Resource professionals who want to support employees' career transition and maintain the reputation of their organization."
Stephanie A. Strozak, SPHR

"*#SUCCESSFUL CORPORATE LEARNING tweet Book04: Career Transition Training and Services That Work in Today's Environment* is an excellent how-to guide for CEOs, managers, and HR professionals for handling downsizing with compassion and integrity. It provides pertinent information on the benefits of career transition services and useful tips for managing staff who survive the layoff. An important reference for any business!"
Andrea D. Trent, SPHR, Consultant, HRBizPartner

Acknowledgments

I'd like to thank Mitchell Levy for being so receptive to my ideas and helping me turn those ideas into realities and Diane Vo, THiNKaha's amazing Production Manager, for keeping me focused and on track during every phase of this project.

Barbara Safani

I have to acknowledge Barbara Safani. She is an amazing co-author to work with. Bright, very capable, fun to work with and above all else, says what she'll do and does what she says...an attribute in a person that's highly regarded in my book. She makes every project we work on together a breeze. If you have an opportunity to work with her, please take it...you won't be disappointed.

Mitchell Levy

Why We Wrote This Book

After working with clients who were the victims of a downsizing for close to a decade, Barbara has seen her share of downsizings handled well and those handled poorly. When done correctly, a downsizing can be managed in a way that supports the employee's career transition and preserves the reputation of the company. When done incorrectly, a downsizing can ruin a person's self esteem, disrupt the productivity of the remaining employees, damage a company's reputation, and even cause financial hardship and costly litigation for the company.

We wrote this book to help employers learn how to manage a downsizing strategically, economically, and compassionately. Our goal is to give employers tools and tactics to make the process manageable while helping displaced employees transition to new careers efficiently and successfully.

Barbara Safani (*@barbarasafani*)

LinkedIn: **http://www.linkedin.com/in/barbarasafani**
Facebook: **http://www.facebook.com/careersolvers**
Website: **http://www.careersolvers.com**
Blog: **http://www.careersolvers.com/blog**
E-mail: **info@careersolvers.com**

Mitchell Levy (*@HappyAbout*)

LinkedIn: **http://www.linkedin.com/in/mitchelllevy**
Website: **http://www.happyabout.com**
E-mail: **mitchell.levy@happyabout.info**

How to Read a THiNKaha® Book
A Note from the Publisher

The THiNKaha series is the CliffsNotes of the 21st century. The value of these books is that they are contextual in nature. Although the actual words won't change, their meaning will change every time you read one as your context will change. Here's how to read one of these books and have it work for you.

1. Read a THiNKaha book (these slim and handy books should only take approximately 15–20 minutes of your time!) and write down one to three "aha" moments you had whilst reading it.

   a. "Aha" moments are looked at as "actionable" moments—think of a specific project you're working on, an event, a sales deal, a personal issue, etc. and see how the ahas in this book can inspire your own "aha!" moment, something that you can specifically act on.

2. Mark your calendar to re-read this book again in 30 days.

3. Repeat step #1 and write down one to three "aha" moments that grab you this time. I guarantee that they will be different than the first time.

After reading a THiNKaha book, writing down your "aha" moments, re-reading it, and writing down more "aha" moments, you'll begin to see how these books contextually apply to you. THiNKaha books advocate for continuous, life-long learning. They will help you transform your "aha" moments into actionable items with tangible results until you no longer have to say "aha!" to these moments—they'll become part of your daily practice as you continue to grow and learn.

As CEO of THiNKaha, I definitely practice what I preach. I read *#CORPORATE CULTURE tweet*, *#LEADERSHIP tweet*, and *#TEAMWORK tweet* once a month and take away two to three different action items from each of them every time. Please e-mail me your "aha" moments.

Mitchell Levy, CEO
publisher@thinkaha.com

THiNKaha ®

Career Transition Training and Services That Work in Today's Environment

Contents

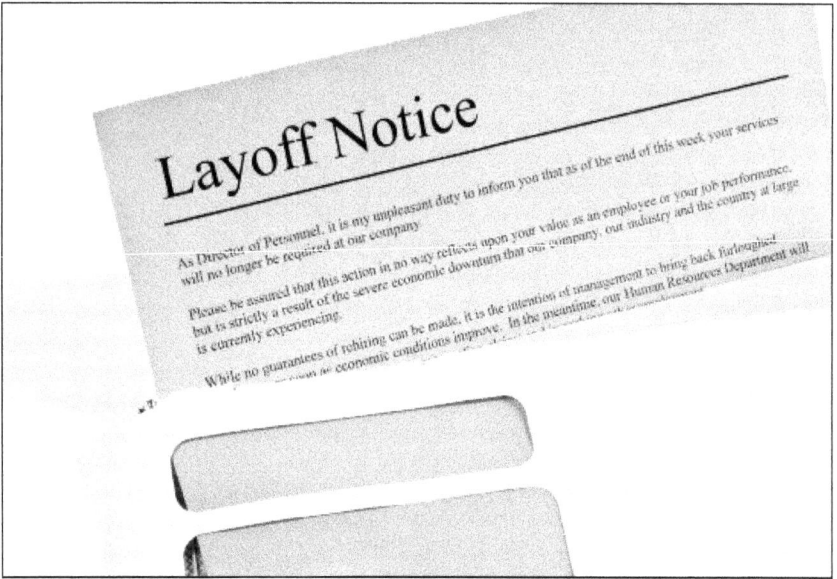

Layoff Notice

As Director of Personnel, it is my unpleasant duty to inform you that as of the end of this week your services will no longer be required at our company.

Please be assured that this action in no way reflects upon your value as an employee or your job performance, but is strictly a result of the severe economic downturn that our company, our industry and the country at large is currently experiencing.

While no guarantees of rehiring can be made, it is the intention of management to bring back furloughed .... as economic conditions improve. In the meantime, our Human Resources Department will

Section I
What Is Career Transition, Who Uses It, and What Are the Benefits?

Career transition services and training used to be a service provided almost exclusively to senior executives when a company realized the executive was not a good fit for the job or the organization and needed to be transitioned out. Providers were often retained on the "QT" to help the executive make a quiet exit, ease the transition process, and give the executive an office with administrative support so they could have a home base for managing their job search.

Today, career transition firms are retained by many companies to support their changing business needs which may include staff reductions. It is not unusual for someone to be downsized during their professional career through no fault of their own and career transition services have become an expected benefit in many organizations. The career transition model of today is transparent and proactive and focuses on giving the departed employee the knowledge and tools necessary to conduct an effective search and land a new job quickly. This section explains the career transition model and its benefits in more detail.

1

Corporate downsizings are sometimes inevitable. Being prepared for them is a competitive advantage.

2

A downsizing can negatively impact your business if the process is not managed properly.

3

"Career transition" describes efforts made by a downsizing company to help former employees through the transition to new jobs.

4

Career transition can be a recruiting tool since it is a benefit many job seekers look for in a company they are considering working for.

5

By offering transition services, you position your firm as a good corporate citizen and a desirable place to work.

6

The company image you present is critical and there is great value in promoting the organization's commitment to displaced employees.

7

Career transition services
began 30+ years ago when
businesses found a need to
help reduce the trauma
of job loss.

8

Companies need to respond to changing business, economic and political realities, outsourcing solutions, and workforce demographics.

9

A downsizing can lower operating costs, speed decision making, improve communication, or improve efficiency and productivity.

10

Downsizings can lead to changes in organizational culture, loss of talent and skill sets, legal ramifications, and reputation damage.

11

More than 2/3 of 265 US employers with layoffs offered transition services in the past 2 years.[1]

_____

1. Susan M. Heathfield, "Outplacement Is a Service for Laid Off Employees," About.com, accessed August 29, 2009, http://bit.ly/HR_Outplacement.

12

According to the EEOC, workplace discrimination lawsuits in 2010 were the highest ever in its 45 year history.[2]

2. Lori A. Higuera and Carrie Pixler Ryerson, "2010 EEOC Statistics: Second Consecutive Year of Record High Discrimination Claims," *Fennemore Craig Law Firm*, January 11, 2011, http://www.fclaw.com/newsletter/newsletter.cfm?id=1058.

13

Studies reveal companies offering transition services achieve gains in engagement, recruitment cycle, cost per hire, and referrals.

14

Without third party involvement, the stress of a downsizing can compromise a manager's effectiveness in his/her regular role.

15

Career transition manages the needs of the displaced worker and contributes to a continued positive image for the company.

16

Career transition is a cost-effective strategy that can accelerate a former employee's return to work & trim unemployment insurance costs.

17

By offering transition services
and training, you may reduce
the likelihood of lawsuits filed
by displaced employees.

18

Career transition can significantly reduce the length of time a displaced employee spends searching for a job.

19

Cutting reemployment time also helps cut continued health insurance coverage—a cost that is growing steadily.

20

Career transition services protect the interests of the company and the employees.

21

The average length of time a laid-off worker remains unemployed is 6+ months.[3] Transition services can shorten this time.

3. U.S. Bureau of Labor Statistics, "Table A-12. Unemployed persons by duration of unemployment," *Bureau of Labor Statistics*, last modified February 3, 2012, http://www.bls.gov/news.release/empsit.t12.htm.

22

Company news can spread quickly via social media. By offering transition services you may mitigate negative social media messages.

23

Remain cognizant of the impact a downsizing has on your workforce and your public image.

24

Being open with employees, customers, and other social media fans can make a layoff less painful for everyone involved.

25

Social media sites like Facebook and Twitter make it easy to bad mouth a company or spread news of a downsizing in seconds.

26

1/3 of people know a former colleague who wrote disparaging remarks about an employer on the Internet.[4]

4. James Adonis, "Word of (bad) mouth," *Work in Progress* (*The Sydney Morning Herald* blog), September 23, 2011, http://bit.ly/n2fhY2.

27

A damaged reputation spurred by disgruntled employees following a downsizing may make it harder to attract and keep top talent.

28

Show transparency and compassion—eliminate rumors by tweeting and blogging about why a layoff is needed.

29

Investment in a robust transition program is like an investment in an insurance policy.

30

At the simplest and most human level, offering transition services and training is the right thing to do.

Section II
How Career Transition Can Help Newly Displaced Employees

Many of us are used to hiring professionals for certain services we don't consider our core area of expertise. We pay others to cut our hair, prepare our income taxes, and build our homes. When we are dealing with a life-changing event such as job loss, it often makes sense to leave the heavy lifting to a firm that specializes in career transition. This section offers the business rationale for partnering with one or more transition entities following a layoff or restructuring initiative.

31

Psychologists say that job loss can be one of life's most difficult events.

32

Displaced employees may undergo a grieving process similar to what one goes through following the death of a loved one or a divorce.

33

Much of a person's self-esteem can be wrapped up in their work.

34

In many companies career transition is seen as a standard benefit akin to dental or health coverage.

35

Emotions run high following a company downsizing. Once the initial shock wears off, a normal reaction to the news is anger.

36

Offering transition services can reduce the level of frustration and resentment many laid off workers experience.

37

Transition services help displaced workers gain confidence in the process, which then translates into confidence in themselves.

38

Offering transition services acknowledges displaced employees' loss and helps to preserve their self-esteem and confidence.

39

During the transition process, provide tools and training to help candidates market themselves effectively.

40

Laid off employees may seek jobs with competitors. If they are bitter, they may reveal information they otherwise would not have.

41

Career transition helps
job seekers stay motivated
and accountable because
they remain engaged in
a professional coaching
relationship.

42

The benefits of transition services greatly outweigh the associated costs; they also offer peace of mind for everyone involved.

43

Working with third party outplacement entities gives displaced employees the benefit of an unbiased ear and a fresh career start.

44

People who are laid off after 10 or 20 years have a lot to learn about job search and, unless they have assistance, may be overwhelmed.

45

Transition success is contingent on the flexibility of the employer and job seeker and an awareness of each job seeker's unique needs.

46

No one makes a career of changing jobs. Most are uncomfortable with the job search process and ill-prepared for the journey ahead.

47

By working on a plan for moving forward, displaced employees have less time to think about their perceptions of the company and the layoff.

48

Using transition services can help mitigate the stress placed on the immediate supervisor who needs to deliver the bad news.

49

Career transition is a learning process. People who are properly trained tend to be more effective when managing their search.

Section III
How to Notify Employees of a Downsizing Effectively and Compassionately

The effect a layoff has on a person is profound. An employee will remember the moment of termination forever, so it pays to prepare carefully and thoughtfully for the conversation. With a little bit of practice and planning, you can make the best of a difficult situation and help ease the transition for both your displaced and remaining employees. This section offers practical tips for planning the notification conversation and ensuring that the day goes as smoothly as possible.

50

Provide training for supervisors on how to respond to employee reactions, emotions, and behaviors during this difficult time.

51

Create scripts and follow-up support tools to help supervisors become comfortable in their notification role.

52

Be clear on why people are selected for a layoff and explain the business circumstances surrounding the layoff.

53

Analyze your population early to determine if anyone would be a good candidate for a voluntary exit or early retirement.

54

Encourage employees to use their own judgment in how they communicate the news via social networking connections.

55

Avoid delivering the news on a Monday morning after a 90-minute killer commute.

56

Giving notification on a Friday at 5 p.m., or before a holiday, is poor timing; it gives the person extra time to stew unproductively.

57

Terminating an employee during the workweek helps them immediately notify unemployment and begin contacting their network.

58

No employee should ever be notified of a layoff via email or social media. Respect employees enough to tell them face to face.

59

Following a downsizing, company executives should be visible and available to listen and answer questions.

60

Show compassion and remind the downsized employee that the layoff was due to a business issue, not a performance issue.

61

Don't engage in small talk. Deliver the message directly but compassionately; give employees time to read the written notice of layoff.

62

Be sensitive to employees'
situations, but make sure they
know the decision is non-negotiable.

63

Don't blame others for
the actions being taken.

64

Don't become defensive, argumentative, or confrontational. It is best not to critique the decision that has been made.

65

Be sensitive to employees' responses. Hearing them does not mean you agree with them.

66

Tell the employee how much you appreciate the work they have done and recognize their contributions.

67

Listen carefully; after the meeting, document anything that could lead to a potential problem.

68

Be available in the next few days to meet with employees if they have additional questions.

69

Pay attention to the small details that can help downsized employees get through the ordeal more smoothly and with dignity.

70

Decide if you should notify everyone in small groups, individually, or one large group (for both exiting and remaining people).

71

Coach all involved in notifying employees on how to physically and mentally prepare; get extra sleep, limit alcohol/caffeine intake.

72

Some remaining employees may be on vacation or home ill. Determine how they will be informed of the downsizing as well as exiting employees.

73

Some employees will cry or feel faint following the news. Have tissues and bottled water in the room.

74

Pre-arrange for transportation. Have a car service available for someone who is exceptionally distraught upon hearing the news.

75

Plan for the person to clear out their desk while their co-workers are not around, but give them the opportunity to say goodbye.

76

Have a plan for where the meeting will be held and how the meeting will end. Logistics can become awkward if not planned ahead.

77

Create a consistent plan for collecting keys, ID cards, and other sensitive materials from the employee.

78

Does the displaced employee have any serious medical issues that could be aggravated by the stress of dismissal? Prepare accordingly.

79

Note if the person has a track record of violence or abusive behavior; if necessary, have security on standby.

80

Give employees time to compose themselves before having to face co-workers.

81

Many are in shock after a layoff and will forget what you tell them. Follow up with a letter detailing their separation agreement.

82

If downsizing many employees on the same day, don't schedule meetings too close together; some employees will need more time than others.

83

Have a contact from your transition firm onsite following the termination meeting to answer questions about the service.

84

Review and rehearse talking points prior to the employee termination meeting. Be familiar with the key points of the separation package.

85

Don't assume personal responsibility for the termination. Remember that it is a business decision.

86

Document reasons for reductions in case an employee challenges who was let go.

87

Review who is being downsized and analyze race, sex, and age to ensure the cuts don't create an unintentional adverse impact.

88

If you have 100+ workers, you may be subject to the WARN Act and may be required to give employees 60 days advance notice.[5]

5. The Worker Adjustment and Retraining Notification Act (WARN Act) is a federal law that requires certain employers to give advance notice of significant layoffs to the employees and others.

89

Keep in touch with displaced workers in case business picks up in the future and there is an opportunity to rehire.

90

Have a third party service conduct exit interviews to uncover employee reactions to the layoff. Determine how the process could improve.

91

Give employees a good reference if they deserve one. Giving a positive reference may be one of the best things you can do.

Section IV
How to Manage Your Layoff Survivors

Frequently when we think about a corporate downsizing, our concerns lie with the displaced employees and our energy is focused on how we can smoothly and compassionately transition them out of the organization. Yet, the employees who are retained by your organization, frequently referred to as survivors, also have immediate needs that must be addressed in order to maintain the company image and worker productivity. This section details challenges and recommendations for managing your staff following a downsizing.

92

Communicate honestly and openly about the future of the company.

93

Research shows that reduced commitment and diminished productivity can linger for a year after a layoff if it is not done properly.

94

Survivors may become preoccupied with the safety of their jobs, or become overwhelmed by the new expectations that may be placed on them.

95

Many survivors of a layoff will feel betrayal, guilt & shock; they may question job security, stability & opportunities for advancement.

96

A downsizing can lead to an increase in stress, a spike in sick days, or a decrease in job productivity.

97

If not handled properly, employees may gossip about their fate or spread misleading or inaccurate information about the downsizing.

98

Remaining employees may be concerned about increasing workloads. Conduct staff meetings to brainstorm ideas for realigning workflow.

99

Use multiple outlets for communicating with remaining employees, including small group meetings, email, and telephone hotlines.

100

Studies suggest that there is an increase in stress-related medical claims among layoff survivors.[6]

6. Nico Dragano, Pablo Emilio Verde, and Johannes Siegrist, "Organisational downsizing and work stress: testing synergistic health effects in employed men and women," *Journal of Epidemiology & Community Health*, 59, issue 8 (August 2005): 694-699, http://1.usa.gov/Rreport.

101

Make personal counseling or employee assistance programs available to your survivor employees who need them.

102

Never tell a layoff survivor he should be grateful and he is lucky he has a job. Not everyone will feel that way.

103

Watch the top 20% of your survivor workforce carefully. They may be the ones most likely to leave following a downsizing.

104

How survivors feel about your organization partially depends on whether they believe their downsized co-workers were treated fairly.

105

Employees will know how their displaced co-workers are treated; transition services can provide reassurance to the remaining staff.

Section V
Alternatives to a Downsizing

Before planning a downsizing, an organization should analyze all alternatives to assess if the business needs can be met without cutting staff. This section focuses on alternative strategies to downsizing that may take the place of layoffs or be used in conjunction with a smaller layoff initiative.

106

Institute mandatory time off as an alternative to layoffs.

107

Freeze salary increases or delay raises.

108

Mandate a hiring freeze for all non-essential positions.

109

Offer early retirement and voluntary layoff packages. This will be viewed less negatively by remaining employees.

110

Take advantage of normal
employee attrition; it will
allow you to restructure the
work flow.

111

Cut salaries, reduce work hours, or implement job sharing. This is a better alternative for many than being downsized.

112

Let contract and temporary employees go first.

113

Eliminate overtime.

114

Explore options for retraining employees for roles in growing business units.

Section VI
What Services Do Career Transition Firms Offer?

The key to a strong transition program is customization. Career transition consultants are trained to work with people across various industries and job functions at all professional levels. A credible firm does not apply a "one size fits all" approach to your displaced employees and works with them on an individual basis to meet their future career goals. This section reviews the general services and goals that you should expect from your service provider.

115

Transition services can help job seekers create effective resumes and cover letters in a competitive job market.

116

Clients can take advantage of proprietary databases of information on companies and decision makers to expedite the search process.

117

Being in a transition program
helps build a support network and
community for the job seeker.

118

Clients can leverage practice
interviews and video role plays to hone
their interview skills before the big day.

119

Many people never negotiate salary.
Transition counselors teach clients
how to negotiate salary based on
experience and market value.

120

Few understand how to network during
a job search. Transition counselors
help eliminate negative feelings
associated with networking.

121

The last time many people looked for a job, social media didn't exist. Transition services help clients craft a strong branded message.

122

Job search is a rare time when you can step back and assess what you do. A transition coach can help you understand your strengths.

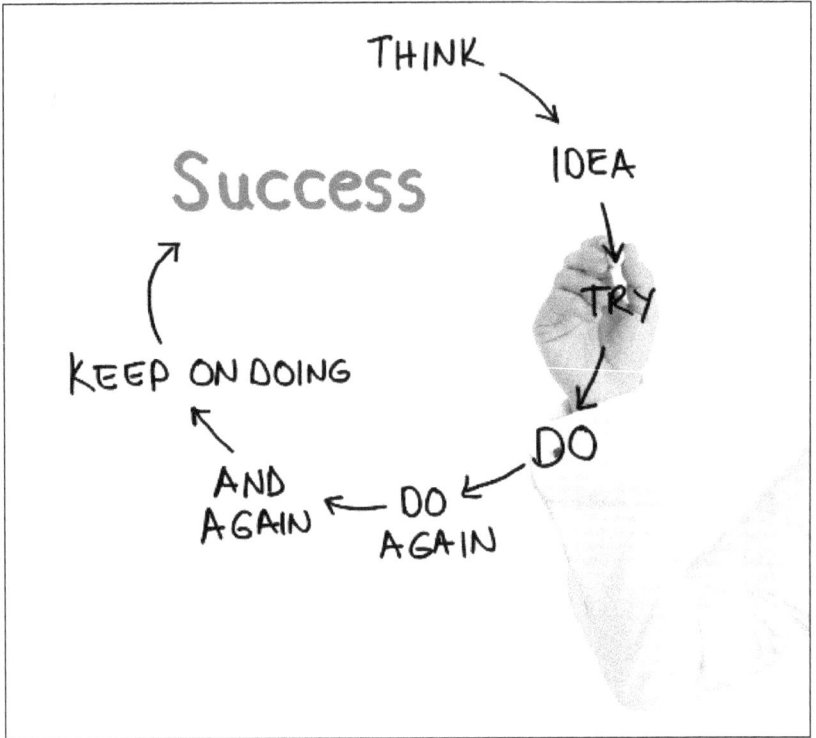

Section VII
Coaching the Downsized Employee

Recently displaced employees are riding an emotional roller coaster and it may be difficult for them to focus. And while it's important for them to talk to friends, family, and counseling professionals about their feelings, it's equally important that they take care of some more tactical tasks that will allow them to move forward. This section contains recommendations for how you can help displaced employees move forward emotionally and professionally.

125

Encourage employees to be honest with their kids about the downsizing and share age appropriate information.

126

Be as available as possible to employees during the transition process.

127

In order to move on, employees need to acknowledge emotions of anger and even denial.

128

Recommend employees take care of any doctor visits now while they still have health insurance coverage.

129

Inform employees of COBRA medical options so they can decide what type of health care coverage is right for them.

130

Suggest filing for unemployment insurance immediately. In many states you can file online without visiting the unemployment office.

131

Extend any company resources you can, such as financial planning assistance or grief counseling.

132

Advise employees of 401k rollover options.

133

Encourage employees to review the severance agreement carefully and make sure severance calculations are correct.

134

Help employees gather copies of performance reviews and customer letters so they can update their resumes.

135

Encourage employees to create or update their LinkedIn profiles and join company alumni groups.

136

Offer a reference or endorsement on LinkedIn. This may prove very valuable later on when the employees are applying for positions.

137

Tell employees what information your company will share about their employment and termination if contacted by a prospective employer.

138

Offer to do an exit interview. The input can help the company better manage employee expectations in the future.

139

Have a grief counselor on-site during the layoff period.

140

Managing a layoff is never easy but finding partners to help the transitioning employee move on will be beneficial to all involved.

About the Authors

Barbara Safani is the owner of Career Solvers, which partners with Fortune 1,000 companies and individuals to deliver career transition programs focusing on resume development, job search strategies, networking, interviewing, salary negotiation skills, and online identity management.

Barbara has been a career expert for CNN.com, CareerBuilder, and AOL Jobs and she has been quoted extensively in major media outlets, including CBS, ABC, FOX, *The New York Times*, *The Wall Street Journal*, *The Washington Post*, *The LA Times*, *Fortune Magazine*, *Smart Money Magazine*, *Money Magazine*, *Oprah Magazine*, and *Cosmopolitan*.

She is the author of *Happy About My Resume: 50 Tips for Building a Better Document to Secure a Brighter Future*, *#JOBSEARCH tweet*, and *Winning Negotiation Strategies for Your New Job*.

Mitchell Levy is the author of twelve business books and the CEO of the independent publishing house Happy About. After earning his MBA from the College of William and Mary, he spent 13 years working for corporations in IT, Finance, and Operations. He then spent 11 years as an entrepreneur creating 13 companies and strategic partnerships, including Happy About in 2005. During this timeframe, he created over 70 courses at various universities, online learning courses, and booked over 500 speakers at large-scale conferences.

Mr. Levy is also partner of the physical networking firm CXOnetworking and sits on the Board of Directors at Rainmaker Systems (NASDAQ: RMKR). Previously, he created four executive education programs at two different Silicon Valley Universities, was the conference chair for four Comdex conferences focusing on business executives at medium-to-large sized enterprises, has contributed to and written over 100 articles, and given over 250 speeches on e-commerce and business.

Books in the THiNKaha Series

The THiNKaha book series is for thinking adults who lack the time or desire to read long books, but want to improve themselves with knowledge of the most up-to-date subjects. THiNKaha is a leader in timely, cutting-edge books and mobile applications from relevant experts that provide valuable information in a fun, Twitter-brief format for a fast-paced world.

They are available online at **http://thinkaha.com** or at other online and physical bookstores.

1. *#BOOK TITLE tweet Book01:* 140 Bite-Sized Ideas for Compelling Article, Book, and Event Titles by Roger C. Parker

2. *#BUSINESS SAVVY PM tweet Book01:* Project Management Mindsets, Skills, and Tools for Generating Successful Business Results by Cinda Voegtli

3. *#COACHING tweet Book01:* 140 Bite-Sized Insights On Making A Difference Through Executive Coaching by Sterling Lanier

4. *#CONTENT MARKETING tweet Book01:* 140 Bite-Sized Ideas to Create and Market Compelling Content by Ambal Balakrishnan

5. *#CORPORATE CULTURE tweet Book01:* 140 Bite-Sized Ideas to Help You Create a High Performing, Values Aligned Workplace that Employees LOVE by S. Chris Edmonds

6. *#CORPORATE GOVERNANCE tweet Book01:* How Corporate Governance Adds Value to Your Business by Brad Beckstead

7. *#CROWDSOURCING tweet Book01:* 140 Bite-Sized Ideas to Leverage the Wisdom of the Crowd by Kiruba Shankar and Mitchell Levy

8. *#CULTURAL TRANSFORMATION tweet Book01:* Business Advice on Agility and Communication Across Cultures by Melissa Lamson

9. *#DEATHtweet Book01:* A Well-Lived Life through 140 Perspectives on Death and Its Teachings by Timothy Tosta

10. *#DEATH tweet Book02:* 140 Perspectives on Being a Supportive Witness to the End of Life by Timothy Tosta

11. *#DIVERSITYtweet Book01:* Embracing the Growing Diversity in Our World by Deepika Bajaj

THiNKaha® Learning/Training Programs Designed to Take You to the Next Level NOW!

THiNKaha® delivers high-quality, cost-effective continuous learning in easy-to-understand, worthwhile, and digestible chunks. Fifteen minutes with a THiNKaha® book will allow readers to have one or more "aha" moments. Spending less than two hours a month with a THiNKaha® Learning Program (either online or in person) will provide learners with an opportunity to truly digest the topic at hand and connect with gurus whose subject-matter expertise gives them an actionable roadmap to enhance their skills.

Offered online, on demand, and/or in person, these engaging programs feature gurus (ours and yours) on such relevant topics as Leadership, Management, Sales, Marketing, Work-Life Balance, Project Management, Social Media and Networking, Presentation Skills, and other topics of your choosing. The "learning" audience, whether it is clients, employees, or partners, can now experience high-quality learning that will enhance your brand value and empower your company as a thought leader. This program fits a real need where time and the high cost of developing custom content are no longer an option for every organization.

"This program has been very successful and in demand within Cisco. The vision and implementation of the THiNKaha Learning Program has enabled us to offer high-quality content both live and on-demand. Their gurus and experts are knowledgeable and very engaging."

- Bette Daoust, Ph.D
Former Learning and Development Manager, Cisco, and Internal Program Manager for THiNKaha Guru Series

Visit THiNKaha® Learning Program at http://thinkaha.com/learning.

Just **THiNK**...

- **C**ontinuous Employee/Client/Prospect Learning
- **O**ngoing Thought Leadership Development
- **N**otable Experts Presenting on Relevant Topics
- **T**ime Your Attendees Can Afford – 15 min. to 2 hrs/mo.
- **I**nformation Delivered in Digestible Chunks
- **N**ame the Topic—We Help You Provide Expert Best Practices
- **U**nderstand and Implement the Takeaways
- **I**nternal Expertise Shared Externally
- **T**raining/Prospecting Cost Decreases, Effectiveness Increases
- **Y**ou Win, They Win!

www.ingramcontent.com/pod-product-compliance
Lightning Source LLC
Chambersburg PA
CBHW071217200326
41519CB00018B/5570